SO-BIP-657

Mapping the Skies

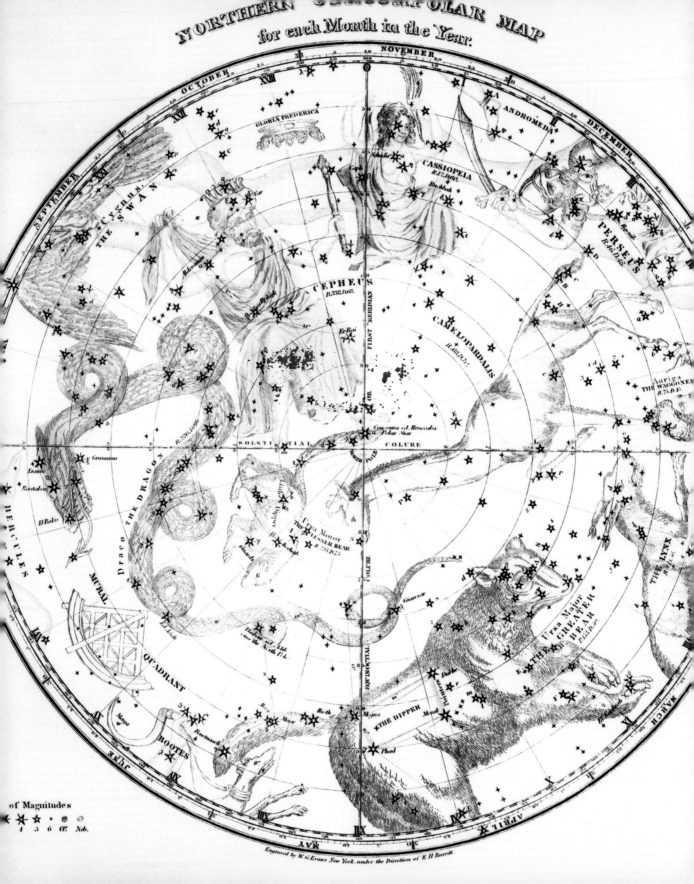

Mapping the Skies

Walter Oleksy

Watts LIBRARY™

Franklin Watts
A Division of Scholastic Inc.
New York • Toronto • London • Auckland • Sydney
Mexico City • New Delhi • Hong Kong
Danbury, Connecticut

Note to readers: Definitions for words in **bold** can be found in the Glossary at the back of this book.

Photographs © 2002: Corbis Images: 41 (AFP), 2, 21, 29, 32, 34 (Bettman), 6 (NASA), 23, 26 (Roger Ressmeyer), 12 (Reuters NewMedia Inc.), 22 (James A. Sugar), 28, 37, 38, 40; NASA: 27 (Erich Karkoshka/University of Arizona), 45, 47; Photo Researchers, NY: 5 right, 42, 43 (Chris Butler/SPL), 14, 15 (John Chumak), cover (John R. Foster), 20 (LOC/SS), 9 (Jerry Lodriguss), 18, 19 (Mary Evans Picture Library), 5 left, 31 (Max-Planck-Institut fur Extraterrestrische Physik/SPL), 35 (NASA/SPL), 24 (SPL).

The photograph on the cover shows the constellation Orion in the night sky. The photograph opposite the title page shows a star map.

Library of Congress Cataloging-in-Publication Data

Oleksy, Walter G., 1930–
    Mapping the skies / by Walter Oleksy.
       p. cm. — (Watts library)
    Includes bibliographical references and index.
    Summary: Explores the tools and technologies that scientists have used throughout the centuries to learn and map the geography of outer space, including those resulting from the space race.
    ISBN 0-531-12031-7 (lib. bdg.)   0-531-16635-X (pbk.)
    1. Astronomy—Maps for children. 2. Astronomy—Charts, diagrams, etc.—Juvenile literature. [1. Astronomy. 2. Space sciences.] I. Title. II. Series.
QB65 .O4 2002
520' .22'3—dc21

2001004939

Contents

Chapter One
Map of the Universe 7

Chapter Two
Stellar Mapping 15

Chapter Three
Better Technology, New Discoveries 25

Chapter Four
Taking a Closer Look 33

Chapter Five
Mapping the Skies Today 43

49 **Timeline**

52 **Glossary**

56 **To Find Out More**

59 **A Note on Sources**

61 **Index**

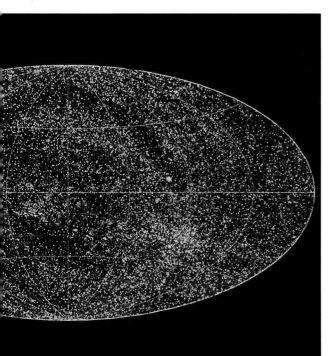

It is sometimes hard to remember that Earth is floating in space, like all the other planets and stars in our Solar System.

Chapter One

Map of the Universe

While the thought of traveling or even living and working in space may seem unreal, the truth is that we are already living on a **planet** in the seemingly endless sky. It's just that Earth is our home and thus familiar to us. That's partly because Earth has been almost entirely mapped. We know its natural features, such as mountains and lakes, and we know approximately where they are in Colorado, possibly, or in Wisconsin.

Also, the Earth is such a comfortable planet for humans. It has a perfect atmosphere, and everything else we need to study, work, play, and enjoy a healthy life. We also feel comfortable on Earth because, unless we look up, we can't see an end to our planet or realize that it is "out there" in space. We don't see the Earth from high above in the sky. We see it from the house or school we're in, or from a baseball diamond or a rock-concert hall.

We're familiar with these places because we've mapped them ourselves by being there. But how would we feel about living on another planet in space? Hey, we've never mapped them! Has anyone? Yes, at least part of some of them.

A Big, Big Universe

Earth is the fifth largest planet in the Solar System, and the only planet known to support life in the infinitely more vast universe. The Solar System, which is Earth's home in the sky, is 10 billion miles (16 billion kilometers) across. At its center is the Sun, by far its largest object. The Sun is in fact a **star**. It shines so much brighter than other stars because we are so much closer to the Sun than we are to the other stars.

Besides Earth, eight other planets **orbit** around the Sun—Mercury, Venus, Mars, Jupiter, Saturn, Uranus, Neptune, and Pluto, along with their **moons**, which are natural **satellites** that orbit the planets. The Solar System also includes satellites, **asteroids**, **meteoroids**, and **comets**, which are chunks of ice mixed with dust and dirt and often referred to as "dirty snowballs." All of these objects orbit the Sun because of its gravitational pull on them. Most of them lie within 5 billion miles (8 billion km) of the Sun.

The Solar System and all of the visible stars are part of the **Milky Way Galaxy**. A **galaxy** is a very large group of stars held together by **gravity**. Our galaxy alone has more than 100 billion stars, and the visible universe has about 50 billion

This photograph shows the southern part of the Milky Way Galaxy.

galaxies. The Milky Way Galaxy got its name because people in ancient times thought the smooth band of starlight stretching across the night sky looked like a trail of spilled milk.

Though we can see many objects in the universe, such as stars and planets, much of the matter in the universe cannot be seen. It is still a mystery to **astronomers**, scientific observers of the celestial bodies, since only its gravitational influence can be observed. This mysterious part, about 90 percent of the mass of the universe, is composed of so-called dark matter. Astronomers believe that dark matter is a kind of cosmic glue that holds the galaxies together and affects the rate at which the universe expands.

Earth is the third closest planet to the Sun, after Mercury and Venus. The three planets farthest from the Sun—Uranus, Neptune, and Pluto—were unknown in ancient times. Whether there are planets beyond Pluto in the Solar System is not yet known.

The Sun gets its energy from nuclear reactions in its interior. It supplies all the light and nearly all the heat in the Solar System. A planet is a smaller body that orbits the Sun or another star and produces no light of its own, but reflects the light of the Sun.

The Sun is 865,000 miles (1.4 million km) in diameter, while Earth is nearly 8,000 miles (12,800 km) in diameter. That makes the Sun over 100 times bigger in diameter than Earth.

Earth is in orbit at an average distance of 93 million miles (150 million km) from the Sun. It completes each trip around

Birth of Earth

Earth is estimated to be 4.6 billion years old based on the radioactive dating of **meteorites**, which are thought to have formed at the same time as the Earth. It is believed that the entire Solar System was formed at the same time in a single series of processes.

the Sun in one year, while spinning on its axis from west to east. It is surrounded in the sky by gases called the **atmosphere**, mostly nitrogen and oxygen.

One of the major things the ancients didn't know about the Solar System—and the entire universe as well—is that it does not always stay the same, but is endlessly evolving. Something new is always emerging. Discovering and revealing these changes and growth is part of the challenge facing astronomers and other scientists who map the skies today.

Why Map the Skies?

From earliest times, humans have been curious about objects in the sky. They wondered how and why the Sun, Moon, and stars appear in different positions in the sky at various times and in different seasons. Where did the objects come from? How did their world come to be?

Later, the ancients mapped the skies for navigational purposes. Desert caravans and ship captains used the positions of the North Star, the Sun and Moon, and other celestial bodies to find their way across deserts and seas. Maps of the skies guided them on all their journeys. Likewise, farmers who watched the stars knew when to plant and when to harvest crops.

Curiosity about possible life on other planets, as well as perhaps living on another planet, continues today. However, the idea of someday colonizing other planets seems a very remote reason for mapping the skies. Astronomers today say that defense is a much more immediate reason for mapping

What Is Earth Made of?

Earth had a very hot, high-density and high-pressure solid inner core at its center, surrounded by a liquid outer core. Circulation in the outer core creates the Earth's magnetic field. Next comes the great bulk of Earth, the so-called mantle. Earth's crust or outer shell consists of the continents and ocean basins, and varies from 5 to 25 miles (8 to 40 km) in thickness.

This illustration is an artistic rendering of what might happen if an asteroid hit the Earth.

the skies. We need to protect Earth from possible impact by asteroids and comets that could do great damage.

Mapping the skies today is focused on learning more about the celestial objects that might come close to hitting Earth. Are they actually on a collision course with Earth? How big are they? When might they hit Earth? With this information, efforts could be made to build the technology needed to deflect such objects. It would be more harmful to blow up the threatening objects because that would create more projectiles that could hit Earth. It would be far safer to somehow move them away from their path of destruction.

Mapping the skies for comets is even more challenging than looking for earthbound asteroids. Asteroids are nearer and could give us years' notice about heading toward Earth. Comets are much more unpredictable, however. In addition, they fall from far out in space, giving much shorter visible notice of their possible impact with Earth.

The constellation Orion is named for a figure in Greek mythology who was a great hunter.

Chapter Two

Stellar Mapping

The ancient Greeks and Romans imagined seeing the shapes of animals and their heroes or favorite gods and goddesses in patterns of bright stars called **constellations**. Legendary stories began to be told about the figures seen in star groups. For example, the Greeks named a group of eight stars Arctos, meaning "she-bear." They associated this constellation, now known as Ursa Major, with the legend of Callisto, a young woman who had been put in the sky in the form of a bear. Individual stars also were worshiped as gods. The Romans called Mars, "the red planet," after their god of war, because its color reminded them of the blood shed in battle.

The first practical use of astronomy was to provide a basis for a calendar, which was needed to plan crop-growing seasons. Farmers would then know the Sun's rising point on the first day of winter and of summer known as **solstices** and on the first day of spring and of autumn called **equinoxes**. Periods of time, such as a month or a year, were determined by astronomical observations.

Egyptian stargazers noted that each year, when the bright star Sirius rose before the Sun, the Nile River soon flooded, fertilizing the land so that crops could be planted. The Chinese had a working calendar as early as the thirteenth century B.C. In about 350 B.C., Shih Shen prepared the earliest-known star catalog, containing eight hundred entries. The Babylonians and Assyrians also were active in early astronomy.

The science reached its highest peak in the ancient world during Greek observations from 600 B.C. to A.D. 400. The Greek philosopher Thales introduced geometrical principles to astronomy. About one hundred years later, another Greek philosopher, Pythagoras, imagined the universe as a series of spheres in which the Sun, Moon, and planets were embedded.

Leading Early Astronomers

The Greek philosopher Aristotle believed the Earth was at the center of the universe. Objects in the sky were part of a celestial sphere, the outer layer containing the stars. Inside the main sphere were fifty-five other spheres, each fitting inside the next. He theorized that the spheres carried celestial objects through the sky in perfectly circular motions around the Earth. His theories remained accepted for two thousand years until the Renaissance period began in the 1300s.

Greek astronomy reached its peak when Aristarchus estimated the size and distance of the Moon and the Sun relative to the Earth. In 260 B.C., he maintained that the Sun, and not the Earth, was the center of the universe. However, this revolutionary notion was not accepted by religious leaders and other astronomers.

Another great astronomer of ancient times was Hipparchus, who lived on the Greek island of Rhodes. He developed trigonometry and used it to determine astronomical distances from the observed angular positions of celestial bodies. He cataloged the positions of more than three hundred stars.

Another Greek, Ptolemy, used Hipparchus's catalog and his own observations to catalog 1,028 stars. His Ptolemaic system was a geometrical representation of the Solar System that predicted the movements of the planets with great accuracy.

Competing Theories of the Universe

Ptolemy disagreed with Aristarchus's theory that the Sun was the center of the universe though. His observations convinced scholars that Earth was the center of the universe and the Sun and planets all revolved around it.

This drawing shows Ptolemy's view of the Solar System.

Ptolemy wrote about the constellations and their astrological legends in his A.D. 150 book *Almagest*, meaning "the greatest." He charted the stars using primitive observation instruments such as a plinth, which is a stone block with an engraved arc used to measure the height of the Sun, and a triquetrum, a triangular rule.

Ptolemy's **geocentric theory** of the universe was the accepted one until the Polish mathematician and astronomer Nicholas Copernicus developed a very different and controversial theory in 1543. He maintained, as did Aristarchus before him, that Earth was not the center of the universe. In his **heliocentric** theory, the Earth rotates on its axis and, along with the other planets, revolves around the Sun. Known as the Copernican system, it became the first modern European theory of planetary motion.

This revolutionary theory caused a great uproar among scientists and religious leaders. Church officials considered it against Christian doctrine to maintain that the Earth was not the center of the universe. At the time, such thoughts could get a scientist burned at the stake as a heretic—a person whose beliefs are contrary to those of religion.

Copernicus believed that all the planets revolved around the Sun.

Helping the Eyes to See the Stars

The **telescope** invented in Holland by Dutch optician Hans Lippershey in 1608 became the most important tool up to that time for mapping the skies. Locating and identifying stars suddenly became much easier. The telescope is a system of either lenses or mirrors, sometimes both, used to gather light from a distant object and form a real optical image of it. The image then could be magnified for closer inspection.

After learning of the invention of the telescope, the Italian astronomer Galileo Galilei built his own, and became the first to use a telescope to study the sky. His telescope had two lenses and was powerful enough for astronomical viewing. It magnified objects to thirty-two times their size.

With his telescope, Galileo proved a number of assumptions about the Solar System were false. For example, he showed that the Moon was not smooth but bumpy and mountainous, and that the Milky Way is not a smooth white band but contains countless stars, some grouped together in clusters. He detected dark spots called **sunspots** on the Sun's surface, and saw what were later found to be Saturn's rings. Discovering in 1610 that four moons orbit around Jupiter proved to him that the geocentric theory of the universe, which says that everything revolves around the Earth, was not correct.

Galileo then accepted the Copernican theory that the Earth revolved around the Sun. But he did

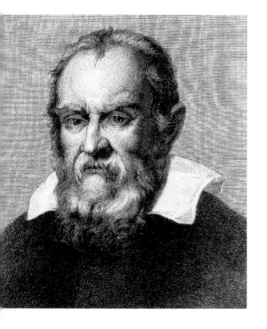

The invention of the telescope helped Galileo learn more about our universe.

not openly support the controversial doctrine until 1613. Three years later, the Catholic Church denounced the Copernican theory as dangerous to Catholic belief. Galileo was summoned to Rome in 1633 and tried as a heretic. He was forced to say that his beliefs were wrong, and he was sentenced to house arrest for the rest of his life.

Another revolutionary discovery in astronomy occurred in 1781 as a result of a survey of the stars and planets by German astronomer William Herschel. Through his self-built 6-foot (2-meter) telescope, he discovered the planet Uranus. It appeared as a disk-shaped object in the constellation Gemini. Calculating its orbit, Herschel found it was twice as far from the Sun as the next closest planet, Saturn. This discovery doubled the known size of the Solar System.

William Herschel studies the night sky while his sister Caroline assists him with his work.

Understanding Telescopes

Refracting telescopes, reflecting telescopes, and telescopes that combine features of both types are the three types of telescopes. A refracting telescope, or refractor, is a long tube with a large glass lens at the top that gathers light from a celestial object. The lens bends, or refracts, the light rays to bring them into focus and produce a sharp image. The image is then

21

The 40-inch telescope at the Yerkes Observatory in Williams Bay, Wisconsin, is the largest refractor in the world.

magnified and viewed through the eyepiece lens at the other end of the tube. Reflecting telescopes are of more complex design. A mirror at the bottom end of a telescope tube gathers and focuses incoming light rays. A second mirror relays the light beam to a place convenient for an eyepiece lens and the observer.

Many of the world's largest telescopes are housed in astronomical observatories at universities. The largest refracting telescopes include the one at Yerkes Observatory in Williams Bay, Wisconsin, with a lens that is 40 inches (102 centimeters) in diameter and one at the Lick Observatory in California with a 36-inch (91-cm) lens. These telescopes represent the practical limit on the size of a lens because the greater weight of its glass causes the lens to sag and distort the images.

A reflecting telescope can be made much larger, because its mirror can be supported all across the back, rather than only at the edge, as required for a lens. For many years, the 200-inch (5-meter) diameter telescope which opened in 1948 at Mount Palomar, California, was the world's largest. Today, a dozen great telescopes surpass it. The largest, fittingly called The Very Large Telescope, in Chile, combines four large mirrors and gathers ten times as much light as the Palomar telescope.

Also, many telescopes have been placed in orbit above the atmosphere. There they are completely free of distortion. They can also observe light of invisible energies that cannot reach observatories on Earth.

The Hale telescope at Mount Palomar was the largest reflector for three decades before even bigger reflecting telescopes were made.

Chapter Three

Better Technology, New Discoveries

Profound changes in concepts of the universe and mankind's place in it evolved during the 1900s because of new technology and astronomical discoveries. These have been—and still are—resulting in major advances in mapping the skies.

One of the most important discoveries was that the universe is expanding. This finding about the universe was the result of investigations by Georges-Henri Lamaitre, a Belgian Jesuit priest and astrophysicist, and Edwin Hubble, an American astronomer.

Studying Albert Einstein's equations involving gravity, Lamaitre concluded that they described an expanding universe. At the time, Einstein himself disagreed with this theory and believed the universe was unchanging. Hubble, meanwhile, became the first astronomer to discover galaxies outside our own Milky Way. This meant that the universe is vastly larger than was previously imagined. It was an even more revolutionary idea than Copernicus's concept that the Earth was not the center of the Solar System.

Hubble spent many years at the Mount Wilson Observatory.

The Hubble Space Telescope

Edwin Hubble's name was given to the Hubble Space Telescope, the world's largest and most sophisticated satellite telescope. About the size of a school bus, it was launched into orbit around the Earth from a **space shuttle** in 1990. The photograph of Saturn shown above was taken by the Hubble Space Telescope.

While working with the 100-inch (2.5-m) telescope at the Mount Wilson Observatory in California in 1929, Hubble analyzed the light of many galaxies in many directions. This led him to announce that they were systematically receding from us and from one another at enormous speeds. Hubble's discovery further convinced Lamaitre that the universe was expanding. He reasoned that by thinking back in time, one can infer that all the matter in the universe must have started out in a super-hot, super-dense state.

Thus, Lamaitre became one of the pioneers of the **big bang** theory, the most commonly accepted theory on how the universe began about 14 billion years ago. By the mid-1960s, after more research and debate, this theory became the most widely accepted explanation of how the universe began.

Advanced Telescope Technology

Most astronomers today do not observe the skies by personally looking through the eyepiece of a large optical telescope. Instead, they record the image with an electronic sensor called a charge-coupled device (CCD) or, less often, with photographic film. Other instruments record the energy and spectrum of the light for analysis.

Objects in space give off **radiation**, or electromagnetic waves, that the eye cannot see, such as **X rays**, and **ultraviolet** and infrared light. Earth's atmosphere absorbs much or all of this radiation. Each of these types of radiation reveals a different aspect of the object that emits the radiation, telling us how bright it is, what it is made of, how warm it is, and how much energy it has.

Astronomers use telescopes equipped with electronic detectors to form images with the radiation. Also, most astronomers use television monitors to see what is being viewed

This ultraviolet image of Jupiter was taken with a space telescope.

Satellite Imaging

Space-age orbiting telescopes help scientists map the universe with far greater precision than ever before. Small orbiting spacecraft called remote-sensing satellites have powerful scanners that transmit photos of planets and other objects in space. They are sent in computer numerical form to mapmakers on Earth.

through the telescope. The telescopes are guided automatically, and the data they gather also are recorded automatically by sophisticated instruments including computers.

Radio telescopes, used in radio astronomy, collect and measure faint radio waves given off by the Sun, other stars, and objects far out in space. The phenomenon was discovered in 1932 when Karl Jansky, an American radio engineer working at a telephone company laboratory in New Jersey, was assigned to find the source of interference disrupting radio calls across the Atlantic Ocean. Tracking down the source of an unknown radio signal from space, he discovered it came from beyond the Earth.

Most radio telescopes work by collecting radio waves with a large reflector called a dish antenna or simply a dish.

Karl Jansky sits beside a machine used to detect radio waves.

29

They look like the satellite dish antennas used to bring in cable and satellite television programs to TV sets.

The reflector focuses the radio waves onto the antenna, which translates them into electric signals. A radio receiver then amplifies the signals and sends them to a computer that analyzes the spectrum of the radio waves or makes an image. The largest radio telescope, 1,000 feet (3,048 m) in diameter, is in Arecibo, Puerto Rico.

Infrared telescopes collect infrared light rays from objects in space. Most of them are reflecting optical telescopes equipped with an electronic device called an infrared array detector. In 1983, an infrared telescope detected rings of dust around the star Vega and other nearby stars that might be solar systems in the process of forming.

Ultraviolet telescopes are used to study extremely hot objects such as **quasars** and **white dwarf** stars. They also are used to investigate how stars form and study the composition of the gas between stars.

X-ray light and its high-energy cousin, gamma-ray light, are found at very short wavelengths. X-ray astronomy has helped astronomers discover or study hot young stars, exploding stars, and **neutron stars**, as well as active and exploding galaxies, and **black holes**.

Scientists launched the first satellite with an X-ray telescope to study X-ray emissions in 1970. This type of telescope has mirrors that resemble a group of short tubes nested within one another. The rays reflect off the inner surfaces of the individual

Space Probes

A space probe is an unmanned spacecraft that leaves Earth's orbit to make scientific observations of the Sun, Moon, other planets, asteroids, or comets. Essential in mapping, space probes take pictures and measure atmospheric and magnetic conditions. Many probes land and analyze soil samples.

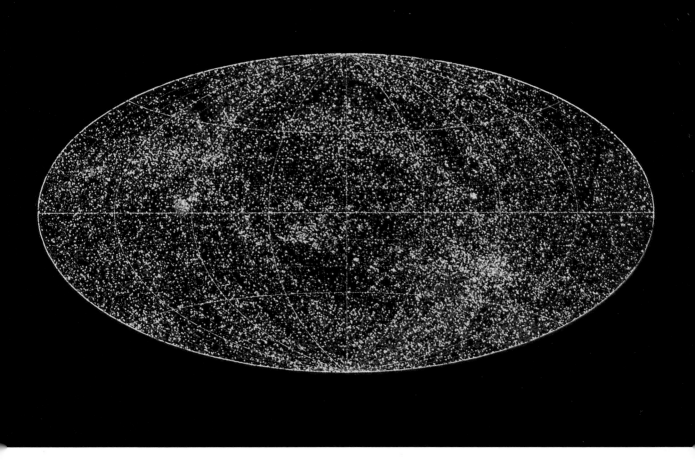

mirrors. By converting X rays to visible light images, scientists have been able to create maps of the X-ray sky.

This photograph is an X-ray map of the sky.

Many high-energy objects in space are strong sources of gamma rays. Gamma-ray telescopes such as that on the Compton Gamma Ray Observatory, a satellite launched in 1991, enable scientists to learn more about some of the least-understood objects in the universe that are strong sources of gamma rays, such as **pulsars** and quasars. In 1997, a gamma-ray satellite called BeppoSAX helped astronomers find the source of a burst of gamma rays—the most powerful explosion ever detected in space.

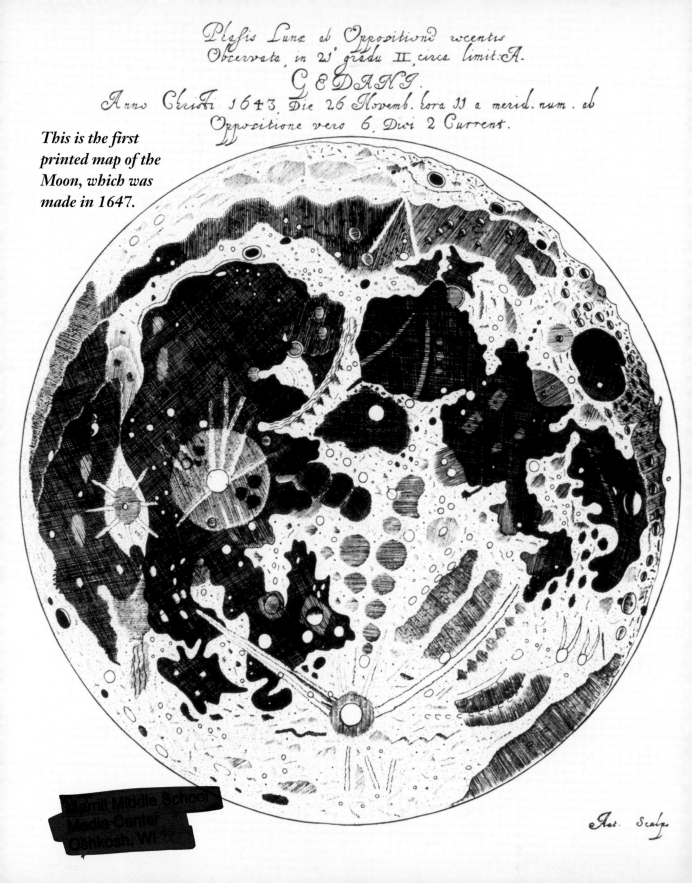

This is the first printed map of the Moon, which was made in 1647.

Chapter Four

Taking a Closer Look

Thanks to space probes, telescopes, photography, and electronic imaging, much of the Solar System has already been mapped. Research is being done to complete our maps of the universe. While astronomers continue to chart the night sky, planetary geologists use similar technology to learn more about the geography of the planets.

33

The Surface of the Moon

Earth's nearest neighbor in space is the Moon. When it comes closest to our planet, the Moon is about 227,000 miles (365,000 km) away. Humans have studied the Moon since prehistoric times and recorded its apparent motions through the sky. Study of the Moon began in earnest when Galileo viewed it through his telescope in 1610. Over the following centuries, the Moon's physical characteristics and surface have been studied telescopically and photographically.

U.S. robot spacecraft surveys of the Moon began in 1958. Three years later, the U.S. Moon research program went into high gear. In response to the Soviet Union launching the first man into space on April 12, 1961, newly elected United States President John F. Kennedy declared to Congress: "Our nation must resolve to put a man on the Moon, and to bring him back safely to Earth before the end of this decade."

The National Astronomical and Space Administration's Apollo program was begun for that purpose. In August 1966, the space agency successfully launched the first Lunar Orbiter. The

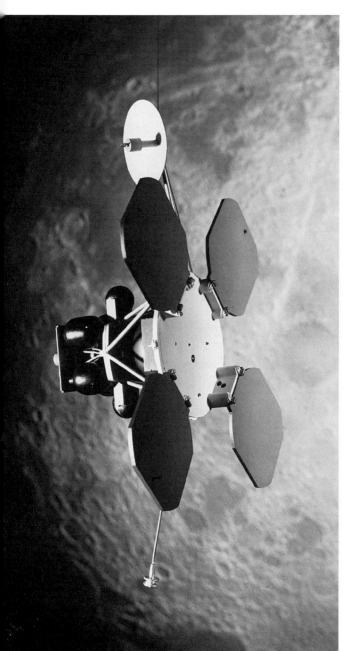

This is a photograph taken by the camera on the Lunar Orbiter.

orbiter took pictures of both sides of the Moon as well as the first photographs of Earth from the Moon's vicinity. Meanwhile, the Soviet Union continued its probes of the Moon. In February 1966, its *Luna 9* probe made the first successful "soft" landing on the Moon, as opposed to crashing, and sent back television footage from the Moon's surface.

Eight years after President Kennedy made his Moon challenge, it became a reality. American astronauts Neil A. Armstrong and Edwin E. Aldrin Jr. descended from the spacecraft *Apollo 11* and set foot on the Moon's surface on July 20, 1969. Five subsequent lunar landings further contributed to the study and mapping of the Moon. They included the use of a Lunar Rover, a jeep-like vehicle that was driven over parts of the Moon's surface. On another lunar mission, nearly 900 pounds (400 kilograms) of lunar rocks were brought back to Earth for scientific study. Moon mapping continues with space probes. As recently as 1998, probes detected indirect evidence of what may be water ice at the Moon's south pole.

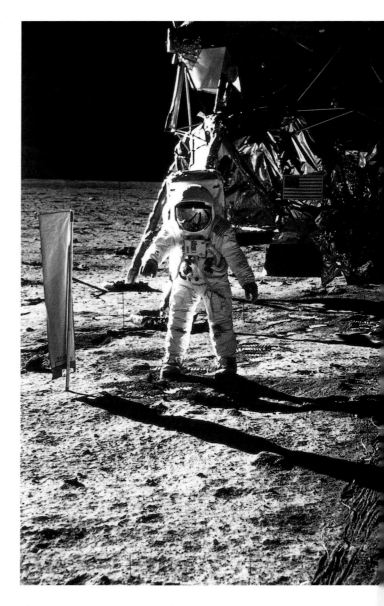

Edwin E. "Buzz" Aldrin Jr. walks on the Moon during the Apollo 11 *mission.*

The Moon is about 2,160 miles (3,476 km) in diameter, a little more than one-fourth of Earth's diameter. On the Moon's surface, the pull of gravity is about one-sixth that on Earth. That is why astronauts wearing heavy spacesuits could bound lightly on the Moon's surface, giving the appearance of floating. Its barren and rugged expanses of rock are familiar to us today, thanks to the lunar landing expeditions of astronauts.

Mapping of the lunar surface shows mountainous bright highlands and large, roughly circular, dark plains. These plains are called maria, from the Latin word *mare* meaning "sea." Early astronomers mistakenly believed the dark plains to be bodies of water.

The Moon was probably formed about 4.5 billion years ago, at the same time as the Solar System. An object larger than Mars apparently collided with Earth. Most of it mixed with our planet, while some ejected material collected in orbit to become the Moon.

Venus

The planet next closest to the Sun, cloud-shrouded Venus, is similar to Earth in size, mass, and age, and thus considered to be Earth's sister planet. However, telescope and space-probe observation has proven the two planets to be quite different. Named for the Roman goddess of love and beauty, Venus is potentially very dangerous. Its clouds look white and friendly, like Earth's water clouds, but they are not what they seem. They consist of droplets of deadly sulfuric acid floating high

up in a deep, thick atmosphere of mostly carbon dioxide. Probes have revealed Venus to be a very hot, dry planet with no signs of life. Most of its atmosphere is carbon dioxide, with some nitrogen and trace amounts of water vapor, acids, and heavy metals.

Mapping of Venus began in 1961 when the United States and the former Soviet Union deployed a series of space probes to study the planet's atmosphere and look beneath its dense cloud cover. United States **radar** mapping from orbit around Venus and through its clouds revealed the surface. Several

This three-dimensional image of the volcano Maat Mons on the surface of Venus was created using radar data.

Radar Mapping

Radar mapping works by sending radar pulses out into space to strike solid bodies or gases. The returning echoes provide information about the roughness and distance of the celestial target. For example, radar signals that were bounced off the Moon showed details of the lunar landscape long before close-up photographs were transmitted to Earth by satellites. Radar mapping from orbit around Venus was an invaluable tool in discovering what lay beneath its dense clouds. It similarly helped Mars orbiters to acquire very detailed altitude maps of that planet's surface.

Soviet landers revealed Venus's surface before breaking down in the extreme heat and pressure.

Space probes have revealed that Venus has a rocky surface of smooth plains, two continental plateaus, large craters, and volcanoes. No small craters have been seen because small meteorites cannot get through the planet's dense atmosphere.

NASA's *Magellan* probe mapped the entire surface of Venus from 1990 to 1994.

The planet's surface was found to be surprisingly young. Only about 300 million to 500 million years ago lava had re-surfaced the entire planet, giving it a new face. Its intense heat, along with a crushing surface air pressure ninety times that of Earth, makes life on Venus unthinkable.

Using radar mapping data received from Magellan, scientists were able to create this image of the planet Venus.

Mars

Farther from the Sun than Earth, the planet Mars—named for the Roman god of war—is about half the size of Earth. With a diameter of 4,200 miles (6,760 km), the entire surface of Mars is about equal to the combined areas of all Earth's dry land. This makes Mars a very large region to explore.

Some early astronomers looking at the planet through telescopes thought the planet's visible dark spots were seas. Lines on the planet's surface were believed to be canals dug by Martian engineers to bring water to populated areas. But a series of space probes by the United States in the 1960s and 1970s showed that there are no canals or signs of life on Mars. It is a barren, crater-covered planet that often has violent dust storms. Very little oxygen is present, no liquid water, and its ultraviolet radiation levels would kill any surface life form.

The Soviet Union was the first to send an unmanned spacecraft to Mars when it launched *Mars 1* in late 1962. The first U.S. probe of Mars, *Mariner 4*, flew past the planet in 1965, reported on its thin atmosphere, and sent back 22 photographs that revealed that its surface was full of craters. Later Mariner fly-by flights in 1969 produced 201 new photos of Mars and also more detailed information about its surface and atmosphere.

In 1971, *Mariner 9* became the first spacecraft to orbit Mars. Two television cameras aboard sent back pictures of 90 percent of the planet's surface and the two Martian moons. They showed enormous volcanoes, a huge valley, and

Mariner 9 *took this photograph of the volcano Olympus Mons, the largest volcano on Mars.*

channels suggesting they had been carved out by large flash floods. Also shown was an intense Martian dust storm.

NASA's *Viking 1* spacecraft, consisting of both an orbiter and a lander, made the first successful soft landing on Mars on July 20, 1976. *Viking 2* landed soon afterward on the other side of the planet. Cameras from both landers revealed rust-colored rocks on the surface, because of the iron oxide in Martian soil.

A main accomplishment of the two Viking landers was testing for the presence of microscopic life. Soil samples at both locations were analyzed for this purpose, but found nothing. In 1997, *Mars Pathfinder* landed on Mars and released a small rover vehicle to test rocks.

On April 6, 2001, NASA launched its latest space-mapping mission, the 2001 Mars Odyssey. It is an orbiter carrying science experiments designed to make global observations of Mars. These would increase our understanding of the planet's climate and geologic history, including the search for water and possible evidence of life-sustaining environments. The orbiter reached Mars on October 24, 2001, and its mission was to extend to 2004.

This is an artistic representation of how the 2001 Mars Odyssey probe would look like orbiting Mars.

Information from satellites and other technology are helping scientists map the surface of the planets.

Chapter Five

Mapping the Skies Today

New and ever more sophisticated telescopes and other technology are helping space probes, satellites, and space stations to gather more information and obtain even more detailed images of objects in our galaxy and the larger universe. Plans are underway for a research base on the Moon, from which future exploration of the Solar System can be conducted.

Another goal of astronomers is a future research base on Mars. One of the main aims of early exploration will be a search for water in some form. If found, it raises the chances of finding past or present forms of microscopic life on the planet.

Many European nations, cooperating as the European Space Agency, as well as India, Israel, Australia, Brazil, and South Africa, have either sent satellites into orbit or launched science-gathering rockets for further mapping of the skies. Canada has an active research program and a communications satellite program. It took part in the U.S. space-shuttle program by designing and building the space shuttle's robot arm. It also built a larger robot arm used on the new International Space Station.

Mapping the Skies Tomorrow

The first of several **modules** of the International Space Station (ISS) was sent into orbit in 1998. Space stations are extremely expensive to construct in orbit and to maintain.

This station will be used to conduct space observations and experiments. To share both cost and space station know-how, the ISS is a global cooperative program involving the United States, Canada, Russia, Italy, Japan, Brazil, and most European nations.

The ISS's purpose is the joint development, operation, and use of a permanently occupied space station in low Earth orbit. Research from the space station is expected to benefit people all over the world through discoveries in medicine, materials, and fundamental science. Through its research and

This illustration shows what the International Space Station will look like when it is completed.

Teens Help with Space-Station Study

Six Gatesville, Texas, high school students and their science teacher, Margaret Baguio, worked with NASA scientists early in 2001 to study and then load biological samples for the space shuttle *Atlantis* to deliver to the International Space Station. It was part of a NASA workshop in which the students learned about proteins and other biological substances that help the human body to carry out important functions on Earth or in space. The samples, in crystal form, remained on ISS about a month, and were then brought back to Earth. Some of the crystals were returned later to the students for comparison with crystals grown in their classroom.

technology, ISS will serve as a giant stepping-stone for future human space exploration.

The United States provided much of the structural framework for the International Space Station (ISS), as well as many of its solar panels. Also contributed were modules in which humans can live and do laboratory work in both the Earth and space sciences. Canada provided a long robotic arm used for assembly and maintenance tasks on ISS. The European Space Agency is building a pressurized laboratory and logistics transport vehicles.

Japan is building a laboratory with an attached exterior platform for experiments and transport vehicles. Russia is providing a module that humans can live and work in as well as solar energy equipment and its *Soyuz* spacecraft for crew return and transport. Brazil and Italy are contributing research equipment.

In December 2000, a crew of one U.S. and two Russian

astronauts aboard the U.S. space shuttle *Endeavour* brought solar-power equipment to the ISS. Then they spent over 27 hours in four space walks installing the new components. The effort marked the successful completion of the ninth mission to the space station.

Still in the construction stage, ISS is already the largest and most complex astronomical project in history. About forty more shuttle missions may be required to outfit the station to full capacity by 2003. The International Space Station is a major step toward charting mankind's possible future of living in space.

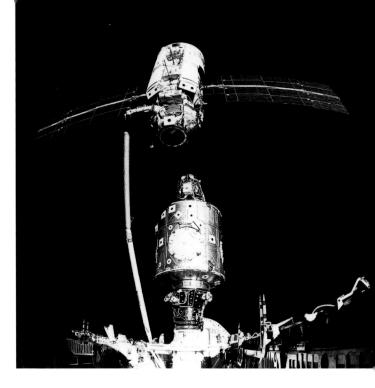

Astronauts prepare to join two modules together.

The Sloan Survey

The most ambitious astronomical survey project ever undertaken, the Sloan Digital Sky Survey (SDSS), began early in 2000. It will systematically map one-fourth of the entire sky, producing a detailed three-dimensional image of the universe. The sky survey will determine the positions and absolute brightness of more than 100 million celestial objects and measure the distances to more than a million of the nearest galaxies and 100,000 quasars, the farthest objects known. This will provide an unprecedented three-dimensional map of the distribution of matter to the edge of the visible universe.

The survey is made possible by advances in imaging technology in recent years. Modern electronic detectors, such as the chips in digital cameras, produce much greater sensitivity than photographic plates. Fast computers and large data-storage systems allow astronomers to take digital pictures of the sky, as well as to process and store the data they collect.

The Sloan Digital Sky Survey is named after one of its major funding organizations, the Alfred P. Sloan Foundation. It is a project of the University of Chicago, New Mexico State University, Princeton University, and the University of Washington, as well as other organizations including Fermilab, the Institute for Advanced Study, the Max Planck Institute for Astronomy, and the United States Naval Observatory.

The SDSS uses a specially built 100-inch (2.5-m) telescope at Apache Point Observatory in New Mexico that is fixed to point directly up at the sky. As the Earth rotates, more of the sky becomes visible above the telescope. Over the course of a night, the telescope images a strip of sky. The telescope will operate on clear nights until 2005, imaging a total of one-fourth of the entire night sky.

Timeline

B.C.	
3100	Egyptians study positions of the stars to create calendars for planting and harvesting crops.
1200s	The Chinese devise a calendar.
350	Shih Shen catalogs the stars.
260	Aristarchus maintains the Sun is the center of the universe.

A.D.	
150	Greek astronomer Ptolemy theorizes that the Earth is the center of the universe, and the Sun and other planets orbit around the Earth.
1543	Copernicus suggests that the Sun is at the center of the solar system, and that the Earth orbits around the Sun.
1608	Hans Lippershey invents the telescope.
1609	Galileo builds a telescope to study the stars and planets.
1781	William Herschel discovers the planet Uranus.
1927	Georges-Henri Lamaitre proposes the big bang theory, which holds that the universe was formed in a huge explosion.
1932	Karl Jansky detects radio noises from space.
1957	The Soviet Union launches *Sputnik I*, the world's first human-made satellite, into space on October 4. The Soviet Union's *Sputnik II* carries a dog into space on November 3.
1958	The United States launches its first space satellite into orbit around the Earth on February 1. U.S. robot spacecraft surveys the Moon.
1959	The first space probe is sent to the Moon by the Soviet Union on September 14.
1961	Yuri Gagarin of the Soviet Union becomes the first person to orbit the

(continued on next page)

Timeline _(continued)_

	Earth on April 12. U.S. President John F. Kennedy challenges American scientists to reach the Moon. Alan B. Shepard Jr. becomes the first U.S. astronaut in space on May 5.
1962	John H. Glenn Jr. becomes the first U.S. astronaut to orbit the Earth on February 20.
1963	Valentina Tereshkova of the Soviet Union becomes the first woman in space on June 16.
1965	Edward White makes the first space walk. The U.S. space probe _Mariner 4_ takes the first photos of Mars.
1966	The Soviet space probe _Luna 9_ is the first to land on the Moon.
1968	The United States launches _Apollo 8_ to orbit the Moon on December 21.
1969	The U.S. spacecraft _Apollo 11_ lands the first men on the Moon. Neil Armstrong becomes the first man to walk on the Moon on July 20.
1971	The Soviet Union's _Salyut 1_ becomes the first manned orbiting space station on April 19.
1973	The United States launches _Skylab_, its first space station, on May 14.
1976	U.S. Viking space probes land on Mars and take photos and soil samples.
1979	U.S. Voyager space probes transmit detailed photos of Jupiter.
1981	U.S. _Voyager 2_ flies pat Saturn, sending back detailed pictures of the planet. The United States conducts the first space-shuttle flight.
1986	U.S. space probe _Voyager 2_ flies past Uranus, sending back detailed photographs of the planet. The Soviet space station _Mir_ is launched on February 20.
1989	U.S. space probe _Voyager 2_ flies past Neptune, sending back detailed photographs of the planet.

1990	The United States launches the Hubble Space Telescope.
1990–1994	U.S. *Magellan* probe maps Venus.
1994	U.S. *Clementine* spacecraft performs first multispectral mapping of the Moon.
1997	U.S. *Mars Pathfinder* space probe reaches Mars and sends back images and information about its soil, rocks, and weather on July 4.
1998	The International Space Station is launched into orbit.
2000	Sloan Digital Sky Survey begins, intending to map one-fourth of the entire sky. A space-shuttle crew of Americans and Russians bring solar-power equipment to the International Space Station in December.
2001	NASA begins 2001 Mars Odyssey mission to map Mars.
2003	International Space Station is targeted to reach full capacity for planetary research.

Glossary

asteroid—a small, rocky object that orbits the Sun

astronomer—a scientist who studies the universe and all the objects and processes in it

atmosphere—the mixture of gases that surrounds a planet

big bang—an astronomical theory of the origin of the universe. It states that a cosmic explosion created the universe 14 billion years ago.

black hole—the area around a collapsed star whose gravitational force prevents everything around it, even light from escaping

comet—a small body of ice, dust, and dirt that orbit around the Sun

constellation—a named pattern of stars in the sky that may resemble an object, an animal, or a mythical figure

equinox—one of the two days when the hours of daylight and darkness are the approximately equal, marking the beginning of spring and autumn

galaxy—a group of stars held together by gravity

geocentric theory—Ptolemy's theory that the Earth is the center of the universe and the Sun and other planets revolve around it

gravity—the force of attraction that pulls a smaller object toward a larger one

heliocentric—having the Sun as the center of the universe

infrared telescope—an instrument for detecting electromagnetic waves from space that are somewhat weaker than visible light

meteorite—a meteor that passes through the atmosphere and hits the Earth's surface

meteoroid—a small piece of debris in space, some of which occasionally collide with the Earth

Milky Way Galaxy—a group of several hundred billion stars including the Sun and its planets

module—a section of a spacecraft that can be disconnected and separated from the other sections

moon—any natural object that orbits a planet

neutron star—the collapsed core of a massive star that has exploded

orbit—the path of a spacecraft or object in space as it revolves around a planet or other celestial body

planet—a large celestial object, such as Earth, that revolve around a star

pulsar—a rapidly spinning collapsed star from which regular pulses of electromagnetic radiation are detected

quasar—a very active center of a distant galaxy

radar—a method of finding position and speed of objects using beams of radio waves

radiation—electromagnetic waves, ranging from radio to gamma rays in wavelength and including visible light

satellite—an object in outer space that orbits planets or other celestial bodies

solstice—a time of year when the length of daylight or darkness is greatest, marking the beginning of summer or winter

star—a ball of hot gases that give off radiation, such as the Sun

sunspot—a strongly magnetic region on the Sun's surface that is cooler and less bright than surrounding regions, thus appearing dark in images

supernova—a catastrophic explosion of a star

telescope—an instrument made of lenses and mirrors and used for viewing distant objects

ultraviolet—electromagnetic waves that have longer wavelengths than X rays and shorter than visible light

ultraviolet telescope—an instrument for detecting electromagnetic waves from space that are somewhat stronger than visible light

universe—everything that exists in space

X ray—very high energy electromagnetic waves

white dwarf—the remnants of the hot core of a star at the end of its life

To Find Out More

Books

Adelman, Elizabeth Fagan. *Rand McNally Discovery Atlas of Planets and Stars*. New York: Rand McNally, 1993.

Asimov, Isaac. *Astronomy in Ancient Times*. Milwaukee: Gareth Stevens, 1995.

Brunier, Serge. *Majestic Universe*. Cambridge, England: Cambridge University Press, 1999.

Miles, Lisa, and Alastair Smith. *The Usborne Complete Book of Astronomy and Space*. London: Usborne House, 1998.

Mitton, Simon and Jacqueline. *The Young Oxford Book of Astronomy*. New York: Oxford University Press, 1995.

Muirden, James. *Stars and Planets*. New York: Kingfisher, 1993.

Whitfield, Peter. *The Mapping of the Heavens*. San Francisco: Pomegranate Artbooks, 1995.

Organizations and Online Sites

Amateur Astronomers Association of New York
http://www.aaa.org
This organization allows amateur astronomers to receive and share information on astronomy.

Kennedy Space Center
http://www.ksc.nasa.gov/
This extensive NASA online site offers information on the history and current projects of the U.S. space program.

Maps of the Solar System
http://maps.jpl.nasa.gov/
NASA's Jet Propulsion Laboratory has maps of the planets in the solar system on its online site, and provides technical information on how the maps were made.

National Aeronautics and Space Administration (NASA)
http://www.nasa.gov
Learn about today's space missions and projects from the U.S. spacc agency.

National Space Society
http://www.nss.org/
This organization provides information on space exploration.

Ontario Science Centre
http://www.osc.on.ca/
This interactive site contains lots of information and games involving space exploration.

Royal Astronomical Society of Canada
http://www.rasc.ca
This Canadian organization's online site is designed for researching and observing planets and other stellar bodies.

Space Telescope Science Institute
http://www.stsci.edu
This online site provides information about the Hubble Space Telescope.

A Note on Sources

I once shared an apartment with a friend who was studying for a doctoral degree in astronomy. One night, we looked up at the sky full of stars and he began telling me that one day man would live on one of distant planets. I asked him not to talk like that, because it gave me the willies to think of being so far away.

But then he said that shouldn't upset me because I was already living in space. It's just that Planet Earth is such a comfortable place to call home. Since then, I became more comfortable thinking about outer space and now I highly recommend it. That friend is now Dr. Eric D. Carlson, astronomer emeritus of the Adler Planetarium in Chicago. He acted as an astronomy consultant for this book.

I learned a lot about NASA's and Russia's space programs over the years, and was just as amazed as everyone else when I watched American astronauts walk on the Moon. I learned more in researching this book, thanks to many good books on the subject and the many Internet sites that are devoted to all the various aspects of space exploration and mapping.

For the early accomplishments in astronomy, I found the most useful books to be *The Mapping of the Heavens* by Peter Whitfield, and *Astronomy in Ancient Times* by Isaac Asimov. The most helpful books on space developments during and since the 1950s included *Astronomy: How We View Our Solar System and the Universe Beyond* by Ian Ridpath; *Stars and Planets* by James Muirden; and *The Usborne Complete Book of Astronomy and Space* by Lisa Miles and Alastair Smith.

The most helpful Internet sites were those from NASA and the Jet Propulsion Laboratory, as well as individual sites devoted to information and images about specific space subjects such as the Hubble Space Telescope and the International Space Station.

It's also exciting to watch documentaries about space science that are shown frequently on cable and satellite television stations such as The National Geographic Channel, Discovery, and the History Channel.

—*Walter Oleksy*

Index

Numbers in *italics* indicate illustrations.

Actos constellation, 15

Aldrin, Edwin E. "Buzz," Jr., 35, *35*

Alfred P. Sloan Foundation, 48

Almagest (Ptolemy), 18

Apache Point Observatory, 48

Apollo spacecraft, 34, 35, *35*

Arecibo Radio Observatory, 30

Aristarchus (Greek astronomer), 17

Aristotle (Greek philosopher), 16–17

Armstrong, Neil A., 35

Assyrian astronomers, 16

Asteroids, 8, *12*, 13

Baguio, Margaret, 46

BeppoSAX satellite, 31

Big bang theory, 27–28

Black holes, 30

Chandra X-Ray Observatory, 44

Charge-coupled device (CCD), 28

Clearfield, Christopher, 44

Comets, 8–9, 13

Compton Gamma Ray Observatory, 31

Copernican theory, 19, 20, 21

Copernicus, Nicholas, 18–19, *19*

Dark matter, 10

Dish antennas, 29

Earth, *6*, 7–8, 10, 11, 28

Einstein, Albert, 26

Equinoxes, 16
European Space Agency, 44

Galaxies, 9–10, *9*, 26
Galilei, Galileo, 20–21, *20*, 34
Gamma-ray light, 30
Gamma-ray telescopes, 31

Hale telescope, *23*
Heliocentric theory, 19
Heretics, 19, 21
Herschel, William, 21, *21*
Hipparchus (Greek
    astronomer), 17
Hubble, Edwin, *24*, 26–27
Hubble Space Telescope, 27

Infrared array detectors, 30
Infrared light, 28
Infrared telescopes, 30
International Space Station
    (ISS), 44–47, *45*, *47*

Jansky, Karl, 29, *29*
Jupiter, 8, 20, *28*

Kennedy, John F., 34

Lamaitre, Georges-Henri, 26,
    27

Lick Observatory, 22
Lippershey, Hans, 20
Luna 9 probe, 35
Lunar Orbiter, 34–35, *34*
Lunar Rover, 35

Maat Mons volcano, *37*
Magellan probe, 38, *38*
Maria (lunar plains), 36
Mariner 4 spacecraft, 39–40
Mariner 9 spacecraft, *40*
Mars, 8, 16, 39–41, *40*, *41*,
    43–44
Mars 1 spacecraft, 39
Mars Odyssey orbiter, 41, *41*
Mercury, 8, 10
Meteorites, 10
Meteoroids, 8
Milky Way Galaxy, 9, *9*, 10,
    20
Modules, 44, *47*
Moon, 8, 20, *32*, 34–36, *34*,
    35, 43
Mount Palomar Observatory,
    23, *23*
Mount Wilson Observatory,
    26, 27

Neptune, 8, 10
North Star, 11

Olbert, Charles, 44
Olympus Mons volcano, *40*
Orion constellation, *14*

Pathfinder spacecraft, 41
Pluto, 8, 10
Ptolemy (Greek astronomer), 17–18, *18*
Pythagoras (Greek philosopher), 16

Quasars, 30, 47

Radar mapping, 37, 38
Radiation, 28
Radio telescopes, 29–30
Reflecting telescopes, 22, 23
Refracting telescopes, 21–22, *22*
Remote-sensing satellites, 29

Satellites, 8, *42*, 43
Saturn, 8, 20, *27*
Shih Shen (astronomer), 16
Sloan Digital Sky Survey (SDSS), 47–48
Solar System, 8, 10, 17, *18*, *19*, 20, 21
Solstices, 16
Soyuz spacecraft, 46

Space probes, 30, 37, 38, 43
Space stations, 43
Stars, 8, 9
Sun, 8, 9, 10, 20
Sunspots, 20
Supernovas, 44

Telescopes, 20, 21–23, *22*, 28–30
Thales (Greek philosopher), 16

Ultraviolet light, 28, *28*
Ultraviolet telescopes, 30
Uranus, 8, 10, 21
Ursa Major constellation, 15

Venus, 8, 10, 36–38, *37*, *38*
Very Large Array (VLA), 44
Very Large Telescope, 23
Viking 1 spacecraft, 40–41
Viking 2 spacecraft, 40–41

White dwarfs, 30
Williams, Nickolas, 44

X-ray telescopes, 30–31
X-rays, 28, 30, *31*

Yerkes Observatory, 22, *22*

About the Author

Walter Oleksy has been a freelance writer of books, mostly for young readers, for more than twenty-five years. He came to that occupation after several years as a newspaper reporter for *The Chicago Tribune* and as editor of three feature and travel magazines. A native of Chicago, he received a bachelor of arts degree in journalism from Michigan State University, then was editor of a U.S. Army newspaper for two years before starting his writing career.

He lives in a Chicago suburb with his best friend Max, a mix of Labrador Retriever and German shepherd. They take frequent walks in the nearby woods and swim in Lake Michigan.

His most recent book for Children's Press is *The Philippines*. His other books for young readers include *Hispanic-American Scientists* and *American Military Leaders of World War II*.

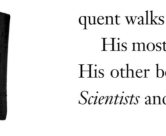